My New Pet

Rabbit

Jinny Johnson

W

FRANKLIN WATTS
LONDON • SYDNEY

An Appleseed Editions book

First published in 2013 by Franklin Watts
338 Euston Road, London NW1 3BH

Franklin Watts Australia
Hachette Children's Books
Level 17/207 Kent St, Sydney, NSW 2000

© 2013 Appleseed Editions

Created by Appleseed Editions Ltd,
Well House, Friars Hill, Guestling,
East Sussex TN35 4ET

Designed by Guy Callaby
Edited by Mary-Jane Wilkins
Illustrations by Bill Donohoe

ISBN 978 1 4451 2200 7

Dewey Classification 636.9'332

A CIP record for this book is available from
the British Library.

Contents

I'm very excited. My mum says I can have a pet rabbit!

I want to know all about rabbits so I can look after my pet.

Here's what I have found out.

A **rabbit** has a plump, rounded body, long ears and big eyes.

Rabbits are **good-tempered** and make great family pets. They are easily scared, so we must treat them very gently.

Pet rabbits usually live for between **seven** and **ten** years.

Wild rabbits live in groups and shelter in burrows they dig in the ground.

A rabbit's coat should be smooth and shiny, with no bare patches.

6

Rabbits like **company** and we've decided to have two so they won't get lonely.

I will look for rabbits that have clean ears, bright eyes and a clean nose. These show they are **healthy**.

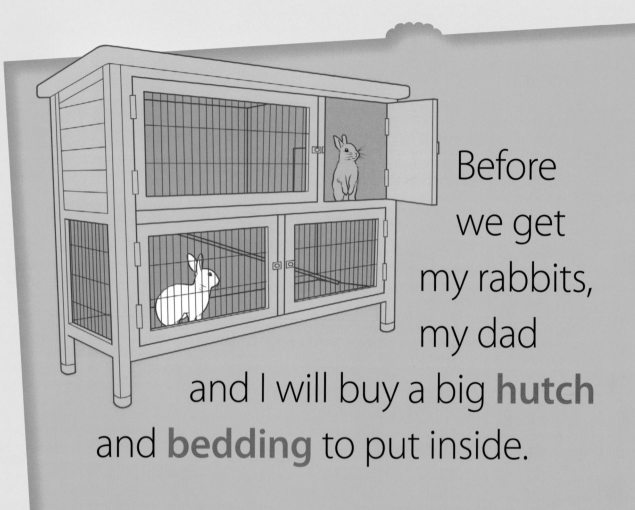

Before
we get
my rabbits,
my dad
and I will buy a big **hutch**
and **bedding** to put inside.

The more room my rabbits
have, the healthier they will be.

We will buy **food bowls**, a **water bottle** and a **grooming brush**.

I will keep my pets in the garden, but rabbits can live indoors, too. Indoor rabbits need a big cage with a plastic base and wire top. I might bring my rabbits indoors if it gets very cold.

I'm going to enjoy making
my new pets' home ready.

*They can hide and
sleep in this area.*

First I will line the floor of the hutch with **newspaper**.

Then I will put in some **wood shavings** to soak up the rabbits' wee.

I will put in **lots** of hay for them to snuggle up and sleep in.

I know it's **very** important to keep my pets clean.

Every day I will wash and dry their food bowls and wash and fill up their water bottle.

Every few days I will take out any wet or dirty bedding. I will sweep out any droppings, too.

Every week I will clean out the hutch and put in clean bedding.

Rabbits like being brushed. Sit on the ground with your rabbit and brush it gently.

Rabbits feed on **plants** and they do not eat meat. They like to eat **hay** and should always have fresh hay in their hutch.

My mum and I will buy some dried food for my rabbits from the pet shop to give them every day.

Rabbits like **fresh food**, too. I will give them treats such as carrots, celery, apples and dandelion leaves. I won't give them lettuce. It's not good for rabbits.

I know I have to be very **gentle** with my new pets at first.

Everything will be strange to them and they might be **frightened**.

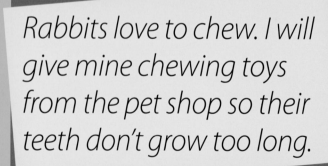

Rabbits love to chew. I will give mine chewing toys from the pet shop so their teeth don't grow too long.

I will let them
get used to
their new
home
before
I try to
touch
them.

Wild rabbits get plenty of **exercise** as they hop about looking for food.

Pet rabbits need exercise too, so I will let my pets out of their hutch every day to run around. I will **watch** them very carefully.

Pet rabbits like to play in cardboard tube tunnels or boxes with holes to run through.

19

Hooray! I have my new rabbits. They are both **female** and they are ten weeks old.

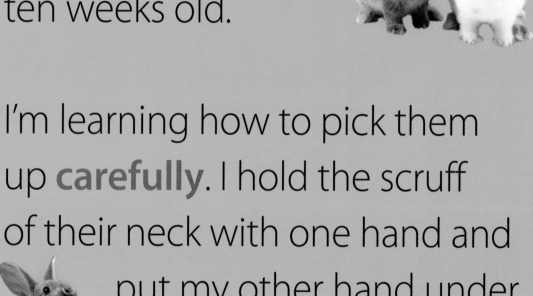

I'm learning how to pick them up **carefully**. I hold the scruff of their neck with one hand and put my other hand under their back legs.

I put my rabbit in its hutch back feet first in case it gets frightened and **kicks** me.

My new pets are going to be very happy – and so am I!

21

Notes for parents

Choosing a pet
Make sure you buy healthy rabbits from a good pet shop or breeder. Take the animals to the vet for a health check. Ask the vet to check the sex of the animals too. Pet shops sometimes get it wrong!

Handling and caring for a rabbit
Show children how to handle a rabbit properly. Teach them to respect animals and always treat them gently.

Health
As a parent you need to make sure any pet is looked after properly. Supervise feeding and handling, especially at first. Keep an eye on the animal's health. Check its teeth and claws regularly and take the pet to the vet if they grow too long.

Words to remember

burrow
A hole dug in the ground where a wild rabbit makes its home.

hutch
A home for a pet rabbit. A hutch is usually made of wood and kept outside.

grooming
Caring for and cleaning the fur. You can buy special brushes for your rabbit.

scruff
The loose skin at the back of a rabbit's neck.

Index